CREED
LEADER GUIDE

CREED
WHAT CHRISTIANS BELIEVE AND WHY

Creed
978-1-5018-1371-9
978-1-5018-1372-6 *eBook*
978-1-5018-1373-3 *Large Print*

Creed: DVD
978-1-5018-1376-4

Creed: Leader Guide
978-1-5018-1374-0
978-1-5018-1375-7 *eBook*

Creed: Youth Study Book
978-1-5018-1383-2
978-1-5018-1384-9 *eBook*

Creed: Children's Leader Guide
978-1-5018-1370-2

Creed: Leader Kit
978-1-5018-2483-8

For more information, visit www.AdamHamilton.org.

Also by Adam Hamilton

24 Hours That Changed the World

Christianity and World Religions

Christianity's Family Tree

Confronting the Controversies

Enough

Final Words from the Cross

Forgiveness

Half Truths

John

Leading Beyond the Walls

Love to Stay

Making Sense of the Bible

Not a Silent Night

Revival

Seeing Gray in a World of Black and White

Selling Swimsuits in the Arctic

Speaking Well

The Call

The Journey

The Way

Unleashing the Word

When Christians Get It Wrong

Why?

ADAM HAMILTON

CREED

WHAT CHRISTIANS BELIEVE AND WHY

Leader Guide
by Martha Bettis Gee

Abingdon Press / Nashville

CREED
WHAT CHRISTIANS BELIEVE AND WHY
LEADER GUIDE

This book is printed on elemental chlorine-free paper.

ISBN 978-1-5018-1374-0

16 17 18 19 20 21 22 23 24 25—10 9 8 7 6 5 4 3 2 1
MANUFACTURED IN THE UNITED STATES OF AMERICA

CONTENTS

TO THE LEADER

Welcome! In this study, you have the opportunity to help a group of learners explore what they believe. They will do so through the vehicle of the Apostles' Creed, one of the most widely used and best known confessional statements in the Western church. The study is based on Adam Hamilton's book *Creed: What Christians Believe and Why* and the accompanying DVD, in which Hamilton explores the book and the Creed in a group setting. In the book and study, Hamilton hopes to help learners—Christians, as well as nonreligious and nominally religious people—explore the deeply held beliefs that have the power to motivate Christians to action, sacrifice, and service.

The study can be used effectively though not exclusively during Lent, the forty-day period of fasting, penitence, study, and spiritual growth that prepares us for the celebration of Easter. Hamilton points out that in the early church during this season, converts were prepared for their baptism on the evening before or very early on Easter morning. The Apostles' Creed was likely meant for use at the baptism of converts. It

is his hope that the study will be a conversation about what Christians believe, why they believe it, and why it matters.

Scripture tells us that where two or three are gathered together, we can be assured of the presence of the Holy Spirit, working in and through all those gathered. As you prepare to lead, pray for that presence and expect that you will experience it.

The study includes six sessions, though it can also be expanded to seven sessions if groups prefer (see below). It makes use of the following components:

- the study book *Creed*, by Adam Hamilton;
- the DVD that accompanies the study;
- this Leader Guide.

Participants in the study will also need Bibles, as well as either a notebook for a journal or an electronic means of journaling, such as a tablet. If possible, notify those interested in the study in advance of the first session. Make arrangements for them to get copies of the book so they can read the Introduction and Chapter 1 before the first group meeting.

Using This Guide with Your Group

Because no two groups are alike, this guide has been designed to give you flexibility and choice in tailoring the sessions for your group. The session format is listed below. You may choose any or all of the activities, adapting them as you wish to meet the schedule and needs of your particular group.

The leader guide offers a basic session plan designed to be completed in a session of about forty-five minutes in length. In addition, you will find two or more additional activities that are optional. You may decide to add these activities or to substitute them for those suggested in the basic plan. Select ahead of time which activities the group will do, for how long, and in what order. Depending on which activities you select, there may be special preparation needed. The leader is alerted in the session plan when advance preparation is needed.

Chapter 2 in the study book explores our beliefs about Jesus Christ. The portion of the Creed addressed in this session may require more time than most groups have available for one session. As leader, you may choose to divide the activities into two sessions. If so, one option is to explore the activities about the virgin birth and Jesus' crucifixion and resurrection in one session, and then to examine the three titles that the Creed ascribes to Jesus in the second session.

Session Format

Planning the Session

    Session Goals
    Creedal Foundation
    Special Preparation

Getting Started

    Opening Activity
    Opening Prayer

Learning Together

    Video Study and Discussion
    Book Study and Discussion
    More Activities (Optional)

Wrapping Up

    Closing Activity
    Closing Prayer

HELPFUL HINTS

Preparing for the Session

- Pray for the leading of the Holy Spirit as you prepare for the study. Pray for discernment for yourself and for each member of the study group.
- Before each session, familiarize yourself with the content. Read the book chapter again.
- Choose the session elements you will use during the group session, including the specific discussion questions you plan to cover. Be prepared, however, to adjust the session as group members interact and as questions arise. Prepare carefully, but allow space for the Holy Spirit to move in and through the group members and through you as facilitator.
- Prepare the room where the group will meet so that the space will enhance the learning process. Ideally, group members should be seated around a table or in a circle so that all can see one another. Movable chairs are best, because the group will often be forming pairs or small groups for discussion.
- Bring a supply of Bibles for those who forget to bring their own. Also bring writing paper and pens for those participants who do not bring a journal or a tablet or other electronic means of journaling.
- For most sessions you will also need a chalkboard and chalk, a whiteboard and markers, or an easel with large paper and markers.

Shaping the Learning Environment

- Begin and end on time.
- Create a climate of openness, encouraging group members to participate as they feel comfortable.

- While the Apostles' Creed will be familiar to many participants, some may never have had the time to explore the beliefs that the Creed affirms. Some may find themselves uncertain about some beliefs. Be on the lookout for signs of discomfort or uncertainty in those who may be silent, and encourage them to express their thoughts and feelings honestly.

- Remember that some people will jump right in with answers and comments, while others will need time to process what is being discussed.

- If you notice that some group members don't seem able to enter the conversation, ask them if they have thoughts to share. Give everyone a chance to talk, but keep the conversation moving. Moderate to prevent a few individuals from doing all the talking.

- Communicate the importance of group discussions and group exercises.

- If no one answers at first during discussions, do not be afraid of silence. Count silently to ten, then say something such as, "Would anyone like to go first?" If no one responds, venture an answer yourself and ask for comments.

- Model openness as you share with the group. Group members will follow your example. If you limit your sharing to a surface level, others will follow suit.

- Encourage multiple answers or responses before moving on.

- To help continue a discussion and give it greater depth, ask, "Why?" or "Why do you believe that?" or "Can you say more about that?"

- Affirm others' responses with comments such as "Great" or "Thanks" or "Good insight," especially if it's the first time someone has spoken during the group session.

- Monitor your own contributions. If you are doing most of the talking, back off so that you do not train the group to listen rather than speak up.
- Remember that you do not have all the answers. Your job is to keep the discussion going and encourage participation.

Managing the Session

- Honor the time schedule. If a session is running longer than expected, get consensus from the group before continuing beyond the agreed-upon ending time.
- Involve group members in various aspects of the group session, such as saying prayers or reading the Scripture.
- Note that the session guides sometimes call for breaking into smaller groups or pairs. This gives everyone a chance to speak and participate fully. Mix up the groups; don't let the same people pair up for every activity.
- As always in discussions that may involve personal sharing, confidentiality is essential. Group members should never pass along stories that have been shared in the group. Remind the group members at each session: confidentiality is crucial to the success of this study.

1.
GOD

PLANNING THE SESSION

Session Goals

As a result of conversations and activities connected with this session, group members should begin to:

- examine the evidence for the existence of God;
- explore what kind of God is revealed in Scripture;
- explore the implications of why our beliefs matter;
- affirm ways we might appropriately respond to a personal Creator God.

Creedal Foundation

I believe in God, the Father Almighty,
creator of heaven and earth.

—*The Apostles' Creed*

Special Preparation

- On a large sheet of paper or a board, print the questions from the Introduction for the opening activity (see below).
- Make available copies of the entire ecumenical Apostles' Creed, as shown in the study book, or display it on a large sheet of paper or a board. Alternatively, plan to project it with a video projector. You will need to use the Creed in all the sessions.
- Also display the lines from the Apostles' Creed that are under consideration in this session.
- Decide if you will do any of the optional activities. For researching scientists' views, there will need to be enough smartphones that each group or pair can have access to one. Or access and print out Internet articles on each scientist. For the expressing gratitude activity, you will need large sheets of colored construction paper cut into pennant shapes, as well as colored markers. After checking with your pastor or someone from the church leadership, decide where and how to display the pennants, and get some tape as well as either string or dowel sticks.
- For the closing activity, post the following statement: If you seek a monument to the architect of the whole cosmos, look around you.

GETTING STARTED

Opening Activity

As participants arrive, welcome them to the study. If there is someone who did not bring a notebook or an electronic device for journaling, provide a notebook or paper and pen or pencil.

Gather together. If participants are not familiar with one another, provide nametags and make introductions.

Invite volunteers to respond to the following posted question from the Introduction to the study:

- What do we mean when we say we believe?

Form pairs and invite them to respond to the following questions, also posed in the Introduction to the study book:

- What are some of your deeply held beliefs or convictions?
- How did you come to hold these convictions?

After allowing time for pairs to discuss, come together in the large group. Ask each pair to comment on one insight that came out of their discussion together.

Tell participants that in this study, they will be exploring what Christians believe, why they believe it, and why it matters, using as a basis one of the oldest and most widely used creeds, the Apostles' Creed.

Opening Prayer

Eternal God, we gather here to explore what we believe about who you are. Open our minds and hearts, that together we may encounter the mystery and wonder of your being in new ways. Grant us the humility and grace to hear other viewpoints that may differ from our own, that we may deepen our own experience of the Holy. In your name we pray. Amen.

LEARNING TOGETHER

Video Study and Discussion

Briefly introduce Adam Hamilton, the book author and video presenter. From his website at www.adamhamilton.org, we learn that Adam Hamilton is senior pastor of The United Methodist Church of the Resurrection in Leawood, Kansas. He writes and teaches on life's tough questions, the doubts with which we all wrestle, and the challenging issues we face today. Participants can learn more about Hamilton and his other books at his website.

In Chapter 1, participants explore what we believe about God, why we believe it, and why it matters. To set the scene for viewing the video, ask participants to look for the origins of the Creed. Following the video, discuss the following:

- What does Adam Hamilton tell us about why the Apostles' Creed was developed?
- Hamilton presents us with the analogy of how a chocolate cake is created. What point is he making in using this analogy? What is your response?

Remind participants that Hamilton closes with some questions. Say that the first two questions will be considered in more depth later in the session. Then ask:

- What questions do you have about God?

Jot down these questions and plan to revisit them at the end of the session.

Book Study and Discussion

Explore the God in Whom Christians Believe

Ask participants to quickly review the first few paragraphs of the chapter under the heading "A Growing Rejection of 'God.'" Discuss the following:

- Who are some of the adversarial "evangelists" the writer cites, and what are their arguments?
- Hamilton suggests that, rather than equating belief in God with anti-intellectualism, violence, or bigotry, these represent

instead various negative impulses of human beings. How do you respond?

- Ask participants to pair up, preferably with a different partner than in the opening activity. Ask one person in each pair to scan silently Exodus 3:1-15 while his or her partner scans Acts 17:16-28, as well as review the content in the chapter under the heading "The God Christians Believe In." Encourage pairs to briefly share the gist of each of the passages, as well as what the writer suggests each passage reveals about the nature of God.

In the large group, discuss the following:

- In addition to describing God as the force from which all things derive their existence, what attributes does Christianity ascribe to God?
- What are the implications of the phrase "God the Father"?
- How would you define the concept of *Imago Dei*?

Examine the Evidence for God

Adam Hamilton uses the example of Lawrence Krauss, author of the book *A Universe from Nothing*, a scientist among others who believe that the universe could exist without an external force. Invite participants to quickly scan the information under the heading "Evidence for God?" to find answers to the following:

- the odds mathematician John Lennox calculates for the self-organization of life on earth;
- astronomer Fred Hoyle's analogy;
- what Hamilton believes natural selection reveals about God's existence.

As volunteers read aloud Psalm 8 and Psalm 19:1-4, invite participants to listen and to think about aspects of the created world in which they see God's glory and creativity. Following the reading, ask them to call out, popcorn style, words or phrases that describe what came to mind for them. List these on a large sheet of paper or a board.

Call attention to the last several paragraphs under this heading, where Hamilton enumerates several reasons why he believes in God. Invite them to jot down the phrase "I believe in God because…," and to take a few minutes to respond to the prompt, listing their own reasons for whether they believe in God. Acknowledge that for some people—perhaps including some of the participants—belief in God may be tentative or may be fraught with uncertainty. Encourage those who harbor doubts to record whatever ideas they have that provide some degree of affirmation.

Explore Why Our Beliefs Matter

Ask someone to read aloud the verses from Psalm 90 included under the heading "Why Faith in God Matters." Point out that in the understanding of science and the perspective of Christian faith, each of us is quite small in the scheme of things. Discuss some of the following together:

- Adam Hamilton notes that a belief in God as both creator and father adds an additional layer of meaning to our insignificance. Why?
- A footnote points out that while God transcends gender, in this study Hamilton nonetheless uses the language of the Creed to describe God. How do you respond to this exclusively male language? Are there descriptors beyond the word *father* that you might choose to expand an understanding of the intimate nature of our relationship to God, and if so, what are they?
- What does it mean to you that you are a child of God, and that others are also children of God?

Affirm Appropriate Responses

Call attention to what the book author affirms as appropriate responses of the creature to the Creator. Ask participants to respond to the following in their journals:

- In what ways do I care for the creator God's earth as an act of discipleship and responsibility?
- What spiritual discipline tools do I make use of in seeking to discern God's will for me and for the whole created order?
- When, where, and how do I express gratitude to God?

Encourage participants to continue to reflect on these questions before the next session.

More Activities (Optional)

Explore the Scientific Pros and Cons

Depending on the size of your group, form pairs or small groups, with at least one participant who has a smartphone in each pair or group. Assign one of the following scientists to each: Steven Weinberg, Sam Harris, Richard Dawkins, Christopher Hitchens, Daniel Dennett, Max Planck, or George Lemaitre. Ask them to research their assigned scientist on the Internet to get information about his views on religion, as well as review the information in the chapter. After groups research and discuss their assigned scientist's views, ask them to report to the large group. Discuss:

- Which arguments about the relationship between science and religion did you find the most compelling?
- Do you personally see a conflict between what science tells us about the way the universe works and what our faith tells us about God? Why or why not?

Express Gratitude with Prayer Flags

Recall Hamilton's comments that the appropriate response of the creature to the Creator is praise, gratitude, and worship. Distribute the prepared construction paper "flags," as well as colored markers. Invite participants to print a word or phrase on a flag that expresses something for which they are thankful to God. Encourage participants to make as many flags as they like. Tape the flags to the length of string and hang where others can see them, or have participants tape each flag to a dowel and stick them into the ground along a sidewalk.

If you like, also suggest that participants take an "Attitude of Gratitude" challenge. People on social media platforms such as Facebook or Twitter sometimes challenge others to post photos or comments that indicate things for which they are thankful. Invite participants to take a similar challenge for the next seven days (or whatever the number of days until your next session).

Explore a Personal Creator God

Form two groups. Ask one group to consider God as father and to brainstorm a list of words and phrases that flesh out what it means to understand God as one with whom Jesus—and us as his followers—has an intimate, personal relationship. Ask the other group to make a similar list as they consider God as creator of all that is.

In the large group, ask participants to read over both lists. Discuss:

- With which of these ways of describing God do you resonate the most? Why?
- Put yourself in the place of the early Christians who formulated this creedal statement. Why do you imagine it was important to affirm both the intimate, personal connection to God's creatures and God's creative power, revealed in God's creation?

Wrapping Up

Ask participants to revisit in silence the questions they discussed in the opening activity, with the addition of the words in italics:

- What are some of your deeply held beliefs or convictions *about God*?
- How did you come to hold these convictions *about God*?

Invite them to reflect on the characteristics of God's nature revealed in the opening lines of the Apostles' Creed. Ask volunteers to respond to the following open-ended prompts:

- Because I believe in God as the creator of all that is and all that will be, I will respond by…
- Because I believe in God the Father, who yearns for the intimate relationship of a parent to a child with all his creatures, I will respond by…

Revisit the questions posed in response to the video. Encourage the group to consider the questions about which they now have more information, which have generated new questions, and which are probably unanswerable. Ask them to continue to reflect on these questions in their devotional times in the coming days.

Closing Activity

Ask participants to quickly review the story with which Hamilton closes this chapter. Have a volunteer read aloud Christopher Wren's obituary. Invite participants to call out examples of monuments to the Creator, the architect of creation. Remind the group to read Chapter 2 before the next session.

Closing Prayer

Creator God, we are stunned by the breadth and depth of your creation. We acknowledge both our responsibility for it and our insignificance in the face of its magnificence. We give thanks, too, that in the vastness of the cosmos, each of us is known and loved by you, as a father loves his child, as a mother nourishes and cherishes the infant she bore. Stir us to respond with awe and gratitude. Grant us discernment as we seek to find our place in your plan. Amen.

2.

JESUS CHRIST

PLANNING THE SESSION

Session Goals

As a result of conversations and activities connected with this session, group members should begin to:

- examine evidence for the existence of the historical Jesus;
- encounter the mysteries and the implications of Jesus' birth, death, and resurrection;
- explore, through a consideration of three titles applied to Jesus, what Christians believe about him;
- affirm that the story of Jesus is our defining story.

Creedal Foundation

> *I believe in Jesus Christ, his only Son, our Lord,*
> > *who was conceived by the Holy Spirit,*
> > *born of the Virgin Mary,*
> > *suffered under Pontius Pilate,*
> > *was crucified, died, and was buried;*
> > *he descended to the dead.*
> > *On the third day he rose again;*
> > *he ascended into heaven,*
> > *is seated at the right hand of the Father,*
> > *and will come again to judge the living and the dead.*
> > > > *—The Apostles' Creed*

Special Preparation

- As noted in the introductory material, the portion of the Creed addressed in this session may require more time than most groups have available for one session. As leader you may choose to divide the activities into two sessions. If so, one option is to plan to explore the activities about the virgin birth and Jesus' crucifixion and resurrection in one session, and then to examine the three titles ascribed to Jesus in the Creed in the second session.

- If you plan to use only one session, read over the suggested activities and decide which ones are appropriate for your group and for the available time frame.

- On a board or a large sheet of paper, print the lines from the Apostles' Creed for this session. Continue to make available copies of the ecumenical Apostles' Creed, or display it on a large sheet of paper or a board. Alternatively, plan to project it.

- Decide if you will do any of the optional activities. For the activity using Joan Osborne's version of the song "One of Us," download an MP3 recording of the song (for a nominal fee) or use a video version from YouTube. Print the lyrics (also available on the Internet) on a large sheet of paper or a board. For the cross-making activity, provide drawing paper and colored markers or crayons.

- For the closing activity, obtain some mildly scented oil, a bowl, and paper towels. If you choose to do the candle lighting instead, you will need a large, white pillar candle, matches, and small individual candles for participants. (Be sure to check for any church rules about the lighting of candles.) If you plan to do two sessions based on this chapter, you might use one closing activity for each session.

Getting Started

Opening Activity

As group members arrive, welcome them. Provide materials for journaling to anyone not having any.

Gather together. If there are any newcomers who were not present for the first session, greet them. Invite one or two volunteers to briefly summarize the highlights of Session 1. Also allow time for participants to report how and for what they have experienced gratitude to God since the last session.

Tell the group that in the late 1960s and early 1970s, the following joke made the rounds among persons in religious studies and still circulates on the Internet:

> Now when Jesus came into the district of Caesarea
> Philippi, he asked his disciples, "Who do people say
> that the Son of Man is?" And they said, "Some say John

the Baptist, but others Elijah, and still others Jeremiah or one of the prophets." He said to them, "But who do you say that I am?" Simon Peter answered, "You are the eschatological manifestation of the ground of our being, the kerygma of which we find the ultimate meaning in our interpersonal relationships.

And Jesus said, "What?"

Tell participants that the issue of just who Jesus was and is, and what this means for our lives, continues to be relevant for Christians today. As the joke illustrates, sometimes the explanations of theologians can make the question less than clear. Invite participants to respond with a word or phrase to Jesus' question: "Who do you say that I am?"

Call the group's attention to the author's definition of *Christology*. Tell them that in the chapter they will consider today, they will explore what Christians believe about Jesus, why they believe this, and why it matters.

Opening Prayer

Eternal God, we gather together to encounter you more fully. Guide us as we seek to come to a deeper understanding of who Jesus was, is, and will be. Grant us a fuller discernment about what it means to believe in Jesus Christ, your only Son, our Lord. For it is in the name of Jesus we pray. Amen.

LEARNING TOGETHER

Video Study and Discussion

In Session 2, the group explores what the Apostles' Creed says about Jesus, what Christians believe about him, and why it matters. Set the stage for viewing the video by asking participants to watch for Adam

Hamilton's explanation of three titles assigned to Jesus and what they tell us about Jesus. Discuss the following:

Hamilton reminds participants that in Session 1, the group explored their belief in God. In this video, he begins by asking the question, "Which God?" What does he mean by this?

- He observes that people often say to him, "I'd believe in God if he would just show himself to me." What do you think God's response would be to that question?
- Hamilton poses the question: "What is it about Jesus, and what he reveals to us about God, that touches you the most?" As you consider the titles Christ, Savior, and Lord, which has the most impact on you as a Christian?

Invite participants to name the questions they have about Jesus. Record these questions on a large sheet of paper or a board, and plan to revisit them at the end of the session.

Book Study and Discussion

Explore the Evidence for Jesus' Existence

Point out that while the author cites evidence from Flavius Josephus and the historian Tacitus in support of the existence of the historical Jesus, he notes that the earliest and most extensive information about Jesus comes from the books of the New Testament. Ask:

- According to the text, what is the consensus as to when the Gospels were written?
- What evidence does the Adam Hamilton cite for scholars' conclusion that there were others who had written about Jesus prior to the writers of the Gospels?

Invite a volunteer to read aloud Galatians 1:11-24. The author tells us that the Book of Galatians was probably written no more than twenty years after the death of Jesus.

After pointing out that the author has referenced all four Gospel accounts in writing his summary of Jesus' life, ask participants to review the material under the heading "A Brief Outline of Jesus' Life." Discuss:

- Which events, actions, or attitudes Jesus revealed are particularly significant to you? Why?

Explore the Case for the Virgin Birth

Point out that only two of the four Gospel writers—Matthew and Luke—include an account of Jesus' birth. Form two smaller groups. Ask one group to read Matthew 1:18–2:23 silently and the other, Luke 1:26–2:21, with both groups generating a list of events in their assigned narrative on large sheets of paper. Also have them refer to the information in the chapter under the heading "Born of the Virgin Mary." After allowing a few minutes, ask each group to report their list. Together, note elements of commonality in the narratives (Jesus was born in Bethlehem; angels played important roles) as well as differences (the wise men only appear in Matthew, the shepherds only in Luke).

Ask participants to review the Adan Hamilton's arguments in favor of the possibility of the Holy Spirit's miraculous intervention in the virgin birth, and invite them to indicate how they respond to those arguments. Discuss:

- Hamilton observes that he once heard a Muslim say that for God to be born in the ordinary human way was simply beneath God. Hamilton disagrees. Why does he contend that it is in this messy detail that we see God's glory?

- What name, used nowhere else in the New Testament, does Matthew use for Jesus? What is the significance of this name for you personally?

Explore Jesus' Crucifixion and Resurrection

Call the group's attention to the lines from the Creed that you posted for today's session. Point out most of the attention in those lines is given to Jesus' death, resurrection, and reigning in heaven. Note that the author reminds us that there is no doubt about the facts of Jesus' crucifixion under Pontius Pilate and that the Gospels all give full accounts of Jesus' suffering.

Invite volunteers to describe the following Jewish understandings about death:

- Sheol, or Hades
- Paradise
- Gehenna
- Shades living in the shadowlands

Discuss the following:

- What is meant in the Creed by the words "descended to the dead"?
- What is the "harrowing of hell"?

Ask participants to refer to the information under the heading, "On the Third Day ..." The author includes accounts of appearances of Jesus from all the Gospels. Invite a volunteer to read aloud 1 Corinthians 15:3-6. Note that this account, like Paul's account in Galatians, is one of the earliest testimonies of witnesses to the risen Christ. Discuss:

- Why is the Resurrection essential to understanding the story of Jesus?
- What does the Resurrection signify? What does it mean to you?

Encounter Jesus in the Title "Savior"

(*Note*: If you plan to add a session, open by reviewing what participants found significant in the exploration of Jesus' birth, death, and resurrection, and then continue with the following activities.)

Ask a volunteer to summarize what Hamilton tells us about the name *Jesus*. Note that Jesus' name can be interpreted as a sign for what he would do. Discuss:

- What is the meaning of the Greek word for sin, *hamartia*? What thoughts to you have about this meaning?
- Being saved from our sins means far more than forgiveness. What else is involved?
- How does Jesus deliver us from giving in to our sins?

Point out that the word *atonement* was an Old English word created to express the meaning of other Greek and Hebrew words that meant "at one ment" with God. The act of atonement reconciles us to God.

Hamilton offers three ideas that may help us understand atonement. Form three smaller groups and assign one of these ideas to each group. Ask them to read the information from Chapter 2 and be prepared to summarize the idea for the large group. After a few minutes, have each smaller group report to the large group. Then invite participants to respond to these open-ended prompts:

- In better understanding the atonement, the idea I found the most helpful was _____ because _____.
- I still have the following questions …

Encounter Jesus in the Titles "God's Only Son, Our Lord"

Hamilton tells us that saying Jesus is God's only son is shorthand for something much deeper. Invite participants to consider the questions posed about what it means that Jesus was God incarnate:

- Was Jesus truly human? How, then, was he also God?
- Did God descend upon Jesus at baptism? Or was he born both God and human? And how is this even possible?

Refer participants to the excerpt from the Nicene Creed. Then ask volunteers to read aloud the verses from Philippians, Colossians, and the prologue to John's Gospel included in the book chapter. Discuss some of the following:

- What is the most frequently used title for Jesus in the New Testament? What does it signify?
- What does it mean that Jesus is referred to as *the* Son of God, *the* Lord?
- How does the author define the term *logos*?
- The author observes that incarnation was not simply about enabling God to walk in our shoes, but allowing God to speak our language. What does he mean?
- What does the author mean by "a generous orthodoxy"?

More Activities (Optional)

What If God Was One of Us?

Remind participants that in thinking about the Incarnation, some people are reminded of the song "One of Us" which was a hit for Joan Osborne. Play the recorded song or the YouTube video and invite participants to read the lyrics. Then encourage them to reflect on the question Osborne poses in the song: what if God was one of us? Ask them to consider the following:

- In the song, Osborne invites us to think about the "what if" of the incarnate God coming to us as a stranger on a bus trying to make his way home. In our contemporary cultural context, what might be some equivalents of the incarnate God coming to us in the form of a carpenter's son born in an animal's barn?

- What do you think might be the result if we saw others as potentially God-bearers rather than "the other"?

Explore the Metaphor of the Cross

The New Testament uses a variety of analogies for how Jesus' death on the cross brings about our salvation. Invite participants to name some of the analogies. Hamilton notes that the cross has spoken differently to him at different times in his life, and he relates a story of a couple facing a serious crisis in their marriage for whom the cross meant different things.

Distribute drawing paper and crayons or colored markers. Ask participants to think about a significant event or experience in their lives, either positive or negative, and to create an image of a cross that depicts what the cross meant to them at that time. They can use drawings, symbols, words, or phrases. Ask a volunteer or two to explain their image.

Write an "Obituary" for Jesus

Ask participants to review the Adam Hamilton's summary of Jesus' life. Then invite them to outline in their journals what they would include if they were writing an obituary for Jesus. Afterward, ask a volunteer to read his or her outline. Discuss:

- What did you include in the obituary that was omitted in the one you just heard outlined?
- *Obituary* is from the Latin *obit*, meaning death. Given the fact that in Jesus' life, death was not the last word, how might we rename this account about Jesus?
- Normally an obituary begins by giving the date of the person's death. How would you deal with the *end* of this obituary?

WRAPPING UP

Revisit the questions that participants posed about Jesus following the video segment. Invite them to name any insights they have had about a particular question during the session. Remind them that they will no doubt continue to ponder questions such as these.

Just as the Passover is meant to be the defining story for Jews, the story of Jesus is meant to be the defining story for Christians. Invite the group to respond to the following quotes:

- "You were born without purpose, you live without meaning, living is its own meaning. When you die, you are extinguished. From being you will be transformed into non-being." (Ingmar Bergman)
- "We are survival machines—robot vehicles blindly programmed to preserve the selfish molecules known as genes." (Richard Dawkins)

Then invite them to respond to the following in their journals:

- As a Christian, I believe my purpose in life is to ...

Encourage participants to continue to reflect on specific ways in which they seek to respond to God's love as revealed in Jesus Christ. Also remind them to read Chapter 3 before the next session.

Closing Activity
Make a Commitment and Be Anointed

Point out that one title for Jesus remains to be considered: that of Christ. Ask a volunteer to define it, and someone else to describe the ancient coronation ceremony by which a person was set apart as king of the people of God. Ask:

- What was the significance of anointing in the coronation ceremony?

Remind participants that in many churches, anointing with oil is a part of the sacrament of baptism, a sign that the person being baptized is marked as God's own. Invite participants to be anointed with oil as a sign of being consecrated for God's service.

Have participants form a circle. Turn to the person on your right and make the sign of the cross on his or her forehead with oil. Pass the oil to that person and invite him or her to anoint the forehead of the person to the right, and continue around the circle.

Remind the group that Karl Barth, when asked if he could sum up his extensive theological work in one sentence, responded with the first line of the hymn "Jesus Loves Me." If you like, close by singing together the song or just its refrain.

Alternative Closing Activity

(If you have added a session, or if you prefer not to use the anointing activity, do the following.)

In the video segment, Hamilton describes the candle-lighting service in his church on Christmas Eve. Though no one can deny that there is darkness in the world, Christians light candles as a symbol of God's presence and action. God sent Jesus to illuminate our darkness and to send Christians out to push back the darkness.

Invite participants to form a circle. Light the Christ candle, and if possible, extinguish the room lights. Light your own candle from the Christ candle, and then light the candle of the participant to your right from your candle. Participants will share the light around the circle until all candles are lit. Stand in silence for a moment or two, then say "Jesus Christ, the light of the world. Amen."

Closing Prayer

Pray the following:

Gracious God, your majesty and holiness is beyond our ability to comprehend. Thank you for sending your Son, Jesus Christ, whose life, words, and deeds communicate to us your boundless love in a language we can understand. For it is in the name of this Jesus Christ we pray. Amen.

3.

The Holy Spirit

Planning the Session

Session Goals

As a result of conversations and activities connected with this session, group members should begin to:

- examine what the Old and New Testaments have to say about the Holy Spirit;
- explore, through a consideration of analogies and graphic representations, the mystery and paradox of the Trinity;
- encounter the working of the Holy Spirit in the church and in individual lives;
- commit to listen more fully for the Spirit's voice and to welcome the Spirit's work.

Creedal Foundation

> *I believe in the Holy Spirit....*
>
> —*The Apostles' Creed*

Special Preparation

- On a large sheet of paper or a board, print the line from the Apostles' Creed that is the focus of today's session. Also continue to make available copies of the ecumenical version of the Apostles' Creed, or project it.
- On two large sheets of paper, print the following: "Old Testament" on one, and "New Testament" on the other.
- Also on a large sheet of paper or a board, draw the diagram from the book of the Shield of the Trinity.
- Decide if you will do any of the optional activities. For the activity in which participants create an analogy or diagram, provide writing and drawing paper, as well as colored markers. If you like, provide other materials such as construction paper and glue. For the hymn study, participants will need copies of hymnals or copies of the lyrics.
- Locate the hymn "Spirit of the Living God" in a hymnal or on the Internet and arrange for accompaniment. Alternatively, choose a version on YouTube.

GETTING STARTED

Opening Activity

As participants arrive, welcome them to the study and provide materials for those who did not bring an electronic device for journaling.

Gather together. Ask volunteers to report on their reflections since the last session on specific ways they seek to respond to God's love as revealed in Jesus Christ.

Invite participants to quickly review the information in the chapter under the first heading, "The Voices That Influence and Shape Us." Then ask them to respond to the following:

- What voices do you listen to?
- Which of these voices lead you to become more the person God intends you to be?
- Which voices influence you in negative ways, or act as a barrier to God's will for your life?

Remind participants that in the two previous sessions, they explored the lines from the Apostles' Creed about God the Father and God the Son, Jesus Christ. In this chapter they will consider who the Holy Spirit is, what the Holy Spirit does, and why the Holy Spirit matters.

Opening Prayer

Holy God, we are in awe of your creative and sustaining power. We are overwhelmed with the gift of your Son, Jesus Christ, whom you sent to demonstrate the depth and breadth of your love. We know you have promised that where two or three are gathered together, there you will be also. Now make us aware of your presence with us today as we seek to better discern your active work in our lives. For it is in the name of you, the Triune God, that we pray. Amen.

LEARNING TOGETHER

Video Study and Discussion

Chapter 3 explores what the Creed says about the Holy Spirit, what Christians believe about the Spirit, and why it matters. To set the stage for viewing the video, remind participants that in the Session 2 video, Adam Hamilton used the light of many candles that fill his church on Christmas Eve as a reminder that Christ is the light of the world and that Christians are called to push back the darkness. As they view this segment, invite them to look for how Hamilton uses another light source to explain the Holy Spirit.

After viewing the video, discuss some of the following:

- What challenge does Adam Hamilton say we face with respect to the Holy Spirit's work?
- What light source does he use to illustrate how the Spirit works within believers?
- Hamilton believes the Spirit nudges and guides him. Have you seen or experienced the working of the Holy Spirit in your life? If so, how?
- Muslims and Jews sometimes accuse Christians of being "tritheists." What does this mean? How do Christians answer this critique?

Invite participants to name questions they have about the Holy Spirit and about the Trinity. Jot these down on a large sheet of paper or a board, and tell the group you will revisit the questions at the end of the session.

Book Study and Discussion

Explore Old and New Testament Texts

Invite someone to read aloud the paragraph under the heading "The Voices That Influence and Shape Us" that begins "When we speak about the Holy Spirit...." Call the group's attention to what Hamilton says about the frequent occurrence of the two words translated as "spirit" in Scripture (*ruach* and *pneuma*). Note the multiple meanings these words can have depending on the context. Ask volunteers to read aloud the translations of Genesis 1:1-2 included in the book chapter.

Call attention to the two large sheets of paper, one headed "Old Testament" and the other "New Testament." Invite participants to quickly scan the information under the heading "The Holy Spirit in the Old Testament" and to call out, popcorn style, what they notice about the ways the Spirit worked as recorded in examples in that testament, as well any insights that strike them about the scriptural examples the author gives us. Do the same for the New Testament on the second sheet. Then discuss:

- What are some key differences between the Old and the New Testaments' understanding of the workings of the Spirit?

Ask a volunteer to read aloud again Genesis 1:1-2 and someone else to read Acts 2:1-4 (included in the book chapter). Read aloud the following paragraph from the book chapter yourself:

> I love this imagery for the Spirit—a rushing, violent wind. But notice too the connection to the creation story in Genesis. There God breathed into and filled the man and woman, animating them and giving them life. Here God breathes upon Jesus' followers and fills them and makes them new. This is the re-creation of humanity by the work of the Holy Spirit.

Discuss:

- Hamilton observes that many people seem to be living Spirit-deficient lives. What does he mean? Where do you see evidence of the fruits of the Spirit in the lives of others around you?
- Invite the group to reflect in silence on the following questions: Where do you see evidence of God's spirit breathing new life into your own life? Where do you see the Spirit's work of re-creation filling the church with new life?

Explore the Doctrine of the Trinity

Review with participants the biblical references that seem to point to the Trinity, as articulated under the heading "The Holy Spirit and the Doctrine of the Trinity." Point out that the doctrine is not spelled out by the New Testament writers, nor unpacked by Jesus, which should leave us with a great measure of humility in our statements about the Trinity.

Form pairs. Ask one person in each pair to read the material in the book chapter explaining the analogy of the atom, and the other the material about the analogy of the human body. Allow time for pairs to share the information with their partner about their analogy.

Call the group's attention to the diagram of the Shield of the Trinity that you posted, and ask volunteers to explain the diagram, based on the information in the book chapter. Discuss the following:

- What do you think may be problematic about the following two statements we often hear Christians say: "I am going to pray to God and Jesus"; "I invite you to ask Jesus into your heart"?
- As you consider the two analogies and the diagram, with which way of explaining the Trinity do you most resonate? Why?
- In your own life of faith, is there one "person" of the Godhead to whom you are most drawn? Why?

Encounter the Work of the Spirit

Recall for participants that in the discussion of the video segment, they considered whether they might have experienced the nudging of the Spirit. Invite volunteers to name examples Hamilton gives of times when he has felt the Spirit at work in his own life. Discuss some of the following:

- In what ways does Hamilton suggest the Spirit is at work in our lives?
- He recounts the influence of the Pentecostal movement in the church in the early twentieth century, noting that many Pentecostals believe that receiving the baptism of the Holy Spirit may be evidenced by what is known as "speaking in tongues." What other evidence would you suggest is important to verify the Spirit's working in the life of an individual Christian or a church?

Ask group members to reflect further in the days before the next session on experiences they have had in the past that, in retrospect, might have been whispers of the Spirit. Encourage them to record these experiences in their journals.

More Activities (Optional)

Explore Old and New Testament Passages

Form pairs or small groups, depending on the size of your group. Choose some from the Scriptures below, assigning one to each pair or group:

Old Testament:

- Exodus 25:1-9; 31:1-5
- Deuteronomy 31:1-7, 14-15, 23; 34:1-9
- Judges 14
- Judges 15
- 2 Samuel 23:1-7
- Isaiah 61:1-4
- Ezekiel 36:16-26
- Joel 2:23-29

New Testament:

- Luke 1:5-23
- Luke 1:26-38
- Luke 3:21-22
- John 14:15-31
- Acts 1:1-11
- Acts 2:1-13

Ask pairs or groups to describe how the Spirit is working in their assigned passage. Then discuss:

- What is the primary way that you feel the Spirit works in the Old Testament? in the New Testament?

Create Analogies or Diagrams for the Trinity

Keeping in mind the fact that any analogy for the Trinity or diagram attempting to explain it will always fall short, invite participants to create an analogy or diagram of their own. Participants with smartphones may want to refer to the Internet for more renditions of the diagram.

Provide art materials for those who would like to create a diagram. Encourage them to refer to the book chapter's discussion of the Trinity to guide their work. After allowing time for participants to work, invite volunteers to explain their creations.

Explore Hymn Texts About the Spirit and the Trinity

Distribute hymnals. Form two groups. Invite one group to use the hymnal's subject index to locate hymns about the Spirit. Ask the other to locate hymns about the Trinity. Ask them to read over the lyrics of hymns to discover how each concept is presented. After allowing time for groups to work, debrief in the large group. Discuss:

- Were there new understandings about the Spirit or the Trinity that emerged in the hymns you researched? Any surprises?
- Did any lyrics raise questions? If so, what were they?
- Which hymn texts communicated the most to you?

Invite groups to choose one hymn from the ones they considered. If desired, sing both hymns as a group.

WRAPPING UP

Revisit the questions that participants posed at the beginning of the session about the Holy Spirit and the Trinity. Ask:

- For which of these questions do you feel you have an answer?
- For which questions do you now have more information?
- Which questions remain for you?

Remind participants that the workings of the Spirit and the meaning of the Trinity remain mysteries even to theologians. Encourage them to continue questioning, exploring, and seeking to better understand these concepts.

Remind participants to read Chapter 4 before the next session.

Closing Activity

The Spirit is already at work in our lives but will not force anything upon anyone. We can resist the Spirit, or welcome and invite the Spirit to work in us. Invite participants to name ways they might open themselves to being more receptive to the whisperings of the Spirit. Invite them to reflect in silence on the following:

- In what spiritual practices might I engage to help to listen more attentively for the Spirit's whisperings?
- What voices in my life may be drowning out the Spirit? What might I do to muffle those voices?

Invite participants to sing together the hymn "Spirit of the Living God."

Closing Prayer

Invite the group to pray silently as you say the prayer at the end of the chapter:

Come Holy Spirit, I need you. Breath of God, fill me wholly and completely. Form and shape me into the person you want me to be. Lead me to do what you want me to do. Empower me and use me; speak to me and through me. Produce your fruit in me. Help me to listen to your voice above all other voices that clamor for my attention. Come, Holy Spirit, I need you. In Jesus' name. Amen.

4.

THE CHURCH AND THE COMMUNION OF SAINTS

PLANNING THE SESSION

Session Goals

As a result of conversations and activities connected with this session, group members should begin to:

- examine an expanded definition of the holy catholic church;
- explore what it means to be the body of Christ in the world;
- encounter new understandings of the communion of saints;
- reaffirm a commitment to be the church—a community called to continue Christ's work in the world.

Creedal Foundation

> *I believe in…*
>> *the holy catholic* church,*
>> *the communion of saints…*
>
> —*The Apostles' Creed*

Special Preparation

- Continue to have available copies of the ecumenical Apostles' Creed, or post it where all can see it, either on a large sheet of paper or a board. Alternatively, plan to project it.

- Also print the lines for today's session on a board or large sheet of paper.

- In the center of a large sheet of paper or on a board, print the word *church*. Have available three different colors of felt-tipped markers.

- Decide if you will do any of the optional activities. For the mural, draw a simple cloud shape on a length of mural paper, or draw the shapes on two or more large sheets of paper. Participants will also need several self-stick notes apiece and pens or fine-lined markers.

- Choose a hymn about the Spirit that is familiar to your group. Some possibilities are "Spirit," "Open My Eyes That I May See," "Come, O Spirit, Dwell Among Us," or "Come, O Spirit." Get copies of the lyrics or copies of hymnals and arrange for accompaniment.

GETTING STARTED

Opening Activity

Welcome participants. Provide materials to those who need tools for journaling.

---

*universal

Gather together. Ask volunteers to report on their reflections since the last session. Discuss:

- What past experiences have you had that on reflection might have been times when the Spirit was nudging you?
- How, if at all, did you respond? What was the result?

Call the group's attention to the title of Chapter 4. Ask each participant in turn to respond with the first thing they think of when they hear the word *church*. When everyone has had a chance to give a response, ask:

- Other than the fact that the phrase is a part of the Apostles' Creed, what comes to mind when you hear the words *holy catholic church*?

Ask participants to reserve further discussion of the words *holy* and *catholic* until they have viewed the video. Point out that in the opening sentences of this chapter, Adan Hamilton tells us that an exploration of the holy catholic church and the communion of the saints is in a sense unpacking and clarifying the work of the Spirit. Tell participants that in this session, they will have the opportunity to explore this in some depth.

Opening Prayer

Holy God, we gather together as your church, to explore what it means to be the body of Christ in the world. Guide us as we seek to discern more clearly how we may be empowered and led by your Spirit. Give us insight into what it means to be the continuing presence of Jesus Christ in the world. For it is in the name of Jesus Christ we pray. Amen.

LEARNING TOGETHER

Video Study and Discussion

In Chapter 4, we explore what it means to be the church, the community of believers, and why it matters. To set the stage for viewing the video, ask participants to look for what Adam Hamilton has to say about the phrase *holy catholic church*.

- In answering Hamilton's question to his audience about the kinds of things they've heard people say about church as a whole, what were the responses? What would you add?
- How does he define the words *holy*, *catholic*, and *church*?

Ask the group to respond to the questions Hamilton poses to his audience in the video:

- How does being a part of the church make a difference in your life? in the community?
- When you invite others to church, what do you tell them about why they should come?

Invite participants to name questions they have about what it means to be a part of the body of Christ, and jot these down for consideration at the end of the session.

Book Study and Discussion

Explore Further a Definition of Church

Form three small groups or pairs, depending on the size of your group. Assign to each group or pair one of the following Greek words discussed in the book chapter: *ekklesia, kuriakon, koinonia*. Encourage groups to keep in mind what Hamilton had to say in the video about these words. Ask groups or pairs to read over and discuss what the book chapter has to say about their assigned word.

Back in the large group, as you print each of the words on the prepared sheet, invite those who focused on exploring that word to name words or phrases that define the word or that add additional dimensions to the definition. You may want to use a different color marker for each of the three words and their descriptors. Discuss some of the following together:

- Do these words and phrases describe our congregation? Do we embody these characteristics, at least in part?
- In your opinion, do we sometimes act more like a secular assembly—an *ekklesia* in the broader sense—or are we living as Christ's *ekklesia*?
- Hamilton observes that when people comment that their church does not act as a caring family for its members, he asks them: "What are *you* doing to help it be this kind of community?" What would be your response to this question?
- We seem to have lost the understanding that the church isn't optional, but is an essential part of being a follower of Jesus. How do you respond? Do you think it is possible to be a Christian but not be a part of the church?

Invite one or more volunteers to read aloud Mark 2:1-12. Invite the group to respond to the following:

- What is meant by the term "stretcher bearers"? Where and in what circumstances have you seen stretcher bearers in action in your congregation?
- When have you yourself experienced the ministry of stretcher bearers? When have you acted as a stretcher bearer yourself?

Explore the Church as the Body of Christ

If we are the body of Christ, continuing the ministry of Jesus on this planet, we would do well to look to the Gospels to see the kinds of things Jesus did, and then seek to do those things. Invite a volunteer to read aloud Matthew 9:35-38 (included in the book chapter). Discuss some of the following:

- The assertion is made in this chapter that the church is the continuing presence of Christ in the world. What is the connection between this understanding and the work of the Holy Spirit?
- Hamilton suggests that if you are not regularly asking, "Where does God need me?" and "How can I love and serve others?" then it is possible you are not yet a Christian. What is your response to this statement? How does he relate such a claim to being saved by God's grace?
- At its best, the church is willing to take risks to love people and push back the darkness. Do you think there is risk involved in being Christ's body in the world? If so, how and why?

Encounter an Understanding of the Communion of Saints

Ask a volunteer to define the word *saint* as described in the book, in contrast to the understanding that a saint is one who is canonized by the Roman Catholic Church. Discuss:

- The word *saint* speaks to both a present reality and a future calling. What does this mean?
- How would you define *sanctification*? How is one transformed, or sanctified?

Ask one or two volunteers to describe their understanding of the communion of saints. Discuss:

- Do you believe we are able to commune with those who have died and gone on before us? Why or why not?
- Hamilton describes worship as a "thin space" where we can be close to those whom we loved who have died. Have you experienced this sense of communing with a "saint" who has died? If so, where and when?
- Who is a part of your "great cloud of witnesses"?

More Activities (Optional)

Create a Mural

Ask a volunteer to read aloud Hebrews 12:1-2 (included in the book chapter). Point out to participants that these verses are preceded in the book by a discussion of the meaning of faith, including people in the Old Testament who were examples of faithfulness. Also call participants' attention to the examples in the chapter of the kinds of small sacrifices that ordinary people, "saints," make for the sake of others.

Invite group members to imagine being surrounded by a great cloud of witnesses, saints they have known and loved who have died. Distribute several self-stick notes to each person and ask participants to print the name of one such saint from their lives on each note. After allowing a few minutes, ask each person to come forward and attach each note to one of the "clouds," naming that person. If they like, participants can describe the ordinary sacrificial actions of one or two of these persons.

Explore the Church as the Body of Christ

As one or more volunteers read aloud 1 Corinthians 12:12-27, invite participants to picture their own congregation. Invite them to respond in writing in their journals to the following:

- Our church acts as Christ's hands in the world by_____;
- as Christ's feet in the world by_____;
- as Christ's intellect in the world by_____;
- as Christ's heart in the world by_____;
- as Christ's eyes in the world by_____;
- as Christ's ears in the world by_____;
- as Christ's voice in the world by_____.

Invite volunteers to share one of these ways in which your congregation acts as Christ's continuing presence in the world. Then discuss:

- How am I personally part of the body of Christ? In what ways do I represent Christ's continuing presence in the world?
- Do we as a church find ways to challenge each member and honor each one's contributions? If so, how?
- If we are falling short of challenging all our members, what do you think we might do to encourage others in their ministry?

Apply Descriptors for Church

Invite participants to name descriptive terms and metaphors for the church that could be used in explaining the phrase "holy catholic church." List these on a board or a large sheet of paper. Among these should be "holy," "catholic," "*ekklesia*," "*kuriakon*," "*koinonia*," "family," 'body of Christ," and "Christ's continuing presence in the world."

Invite participants to choose two of these descriptors and to complete this open-ended prompt about each in their journals:

- Our church embodies _____ by_____.

After a few minutes, invite each person to read one of his or her responses. If there are terms no one chose to respond to, ask the group to suggest responses for those terms. Then discuss:

54

- Based on what we chose to respond to, do you think our congregation is more focused on nurturing and sustaining its members or on discerning Christ's will and acting on it in the world? Or do we strike a good balance between acting as family and acting as Christ's body in the world?
- Invite someone to read aloud 1 Peter 2:9. How should we interpret the words "speak of the wonderful acts of one who called you…"?

WRAPPING UP

Review questions the participants posed about the church at the beginning of the session.

Recall that in the previous chapter, Adam Hamilton used a flashlight and power tool with no batteries as examples of a church that is no longer seeking the Holy Spirit's power or inviting the Spirit's leadership. In this chapter he reiterates this belief, observing that the Spirit's power and presence are essential to the church's ability to fulfill Christ's mission in the world.

Encourage participants to make use of spiritual practices they already utilize as times to intentionally invite the Spirit's power into their lives. They might also use a breath prayer, "Come, Holy Spirit," as a way to begin or end those times.

Also remind them to read Chapter 5 before the next session.

Closing Activity

Before singing or reciting the hymn about the Spirit that you chose, ask participants to read the lyrics silently. Then sing or recite the hymn together.

Closing Prayer

Remind the group that in the previous session you used a closing prayer from the book. To end this session, invite them to pray the same prayer together, only as a corporate prayer instead of an individual one:

Come Holy Spirit, we need you. Breath of God, fill us wholly and completely. Form and shape us into the church you want us to be. Lead us to do what you want us to do. Empower us and use us; speak to us and through us. Produce your fruit in us. Help us to listen to your voice above all other voices that clamor for our attention. Come, Holy Spirit, we need you. In Jesus' name. Amen.

5.

THE FORGIVENESS OF SINS

PLANNING THE SESSION

Session Goals

As a result of conversations and activities connected with this session, group members should begin to:

- examine definitions of sin;
- explore three questions to which God's forgiveness is the answer;
- encounter the burden of guilt that can be the result of sin, as well as the power of grace;
- affirm the centrality of forgiveness of sins to the Christian gospel.

Creedal Foundation

I believe in…
> *the forgiveness of sins.*

—*The Apostles' Creed*

Special Preparation

- Continue to have available copies of the ecumenical Apostles' Creed, or post it where all can see it, either on a large sheet of paper or a board. Alternatively, project it. Also print today's line and post it.

- On a large sheet of paper or a board, print this quotation from Karl Menninger:

  The assumption that there is sin…implies both a possibility and an obligation for intervention. Presumably something is possible which can be reparative, corrective, meliorative, and that something involves me and mercy.[1]

- Also print on a board or paper the following statements:

  I believe that human beings are sinners.
  I believe in the forgiveness of sins.

- Decide if you will do any of the optional activities. For the chain activity, you will need for each participant a number of strips of paper about one inch wide and several inches long, as well as pens or fine-lined markers and tape. If you choose to do the renewal of baptism, you will need a small bowl of water and a towel.

- While many regular churchgoers know the Lord's Prayer by memory, persons who are new Christians or who were not raised in the church may not. For the closing activity, print the Lord's Prayer on a board or a large sheet of paper. After the words *forgive us our trespasses* and again after the words *as we forgive those who trespass against us,* leave a space.

GETTING STARTED

Opening Activity

Welcome participants. Provide materials for anyone who did not bring an electronic device.

Gather together. Invite volunteers to report on ways they tried to be more open to the Spirit's working since the last session, through prayer, Scripture reading, or other spiritual practices.

Call attention to the two "I believe" statements you posted. Ask for a show of hands as to who agrees with each statement. Then ask:

- What is the difference between these two statements?

Adam Hamilton finds it significant that the Creed includes the second statement about the forgiveness of sins, with its emphasis on grace. In this session, participants will explore what we believe about the forgiveness of sins.

Opening Prayer

Gracious God, we come together bringing our shortcomings and our flaws, recognizing our need for forgiveness. We acknowledge the burden of guilt we often carry unnecessarily, as well as the resentment we may harbor for hurts inflicted by others. Open our hearts to receive the love and grace you have to offer. In the name of Jesus Christ, your son. Amen.

LEARNING TOGETHER

Video Study and Discussion

In Chapter 5 we explore what the Apostles' Creed says about forgiveness, what Christians believe about forgiveness, and why it matters. To prepare participants for viewing the video, ask them to look for how Adam Hamilton uses a heavy chain as a metaphor.

Following the video, invite a volunteer to read aloud the posted quotation from Karl Menninger's book, *Whatever Became of Sin?* Ask:

- After calling our attention to Menninger's quotation, Hamilton notes that Menninger also observed that "sin is the only hopeful answer." Why does Hamilton consider this significant?

Discuss some of the following:

- Hamilton defines sin using the Greek word *hamartia*, which means "missing the mark." He invites us to consider this: what are some ways in which you see evidence of sin in the world around us?
- He suggests that the Internet has magnified our struggle with sin. What does he mean? What among the seven deadly sins does he identify as the most dangerous?
- How does the chain help explain the power of forgiveness?
- Paul Tillich once said, "Forgiveness is an answer, the divine answer, to the question implied in our existence."[2] What does Tillich mean by this?

Tell participants that during this session, they will consider in more depth the questions: Who needs forgiveness? Will God forgive *my* sins? Must I forgive others? Invite them to name questions they have about forgiveness, and jot these down for consideration at the end of the session.

Book Study and Discussion

Explore Who Needs Forgiveness

In order to explore the question of who needs forgiveness, we must first define just what sin is. Form small groups of three. In each group, assign one of the following to each person:

- *hamartia*
- seven deadly sins
- fruit of the spirit

Ask participants to quickly scan the text to get the gist of what is said about their assigned term. Then each person will summarize the information for the other two in his or her group. In the large group, discuss the following:

- What would you say is the effect of sin on our relationships—both with God and with other people?
- What is Paul's assessment of the power of sin?

Invite participants to reflect in silence on the following:

- When in your own life have you experienced sin as an irresistible power?

Explore Whether God Will Forgive My Sins

Ask someone to describe what has been labeled "Catholic guilt." Call attention to the metaphor of being shackled by sin. Discuss:

- Has there ever been a time when you felt almost immobilized by guilt? What metaphor would you use to describe the feeling?
- Some people who struggle with excessive guilt do so because their conception of God is inadequate. How do you describe God? What or who has influenced how you picture God?

- Hamilton tells us that Jesus is the one who reveals God's character and will, and he briefly reviews how Jesus' life reveals God's nature. What saying of Jesus, action he took, or parable he told can you name that shows you what God is like?
- What is the significance of *aphiemi*, the word used for "forgive" in the Lord's Prayer?

Ask a volunteer to read aloud Psalm 103:9-12 (included in the book chapter). Ask:

- If we believe it is true that God wants to forgive us and release us from the burden of our sin, why is it that some people seem unable to let go of that burden?
- In the book chapter, Hamilton relates the story of participating in the baptismal service of a woman who had been a drug addict who was helped by a ministry called Healing House. She commented that she would now be able to lead by example and teach her kids how to be faithful followers of Jesus. What example are we setting for our children about the forgiveness of sin? about the burden of guilt?

Explore Whether I Must Forgive Others

Invite a volunteer to read aloud Matthew 6:14-15 (included in the book chapter). Point out that when we refuse to forgive others, we are refusing to release them from the chains of guilt and shame and are taking on new chains of bitterness and resentment ourselves. Discuss some of the following:

- The statement is made that forgiving is not the same thing as forgetting. Would you agree? How do you separate forgiving someone for what they have done to you and forgetting it?

- Those who deal with gender violence or child abuse caution against cheap grace—that is, forgiving easily and without requiring the abuser to be held accountable. Are there other times when offering quick forgiveness without accountability may be unwise?
- Hamilton suggests that consequences themselves may be redemptive. What does he mean? Do you agree? Why or why not?

More Activities (Optional)

Create Chains

By creating chains of guilt and then breaking them, participants can experience being released from the guilt of sin. Make available strips of paper, pens or fine-lined markers, and tape. Invite participants to think of actions or attitudes about which they have experienced feelings of guilt—both things they have done and things they have left undone. These can be specific sins that group members have struggled with, or sins all of us commit in thought or in deed. On individual strips of paper, invite them to print a word or phrase that represents those sins. Then have them form a paper chain by taping together one link, then adding additional links to the first.

Ask participants to drape completed chains around their shoulders and to imagine that the paper chain is a real chain. Ask them to imagine being bent under the weight of seventy pounds of chain, finding it difficult to move or even breathe. Allow time for participants to reflect on the weight of guilt they may be bearing.

Then remind them that the word used in the Lord's Prayer for *forgive* literally means "release," and that God is willing to release us from the burden of guilt we are carrying. Invite participants to imagine Christ bearing the weight and burden of their sins on the cross. Then encourage them to break their chains.

Explore Old Testament Passages About God's Nature

In a footnote to the chapter, we learn that the concept of God being rich in mercy and abounding in steadfast love is found throughout the Old Testament. Form pairs or small groups and assign one of the following to each:

- Exodus 34:6
- Numbers 14:18
- Psalm 103:8
- Psalm 145:8
- Joel 2:13

Encourage participants to read the passages in which these verses appear. In the large group, invite small groups or pairs to briefly summarize the context of their assigned verse. Discuss:

- What does this phrase tell us about God in relation to the passage in which it appears?

Experience a Renewal of Baptism

Remind participants that the Apostles' Creed was first written to be recited just before their baptisms by persons who were converting to the Christian faith. As confirmands stepped into the water, they had the assurance that the sins of their past were forgiven and that God was offering forgiveness in advance for sins committed in the future, if a person asked for God's mercy.

Some participants were likely baptized as infants or as small children. While they may not have their own memory of their baptisms, they can experience a renewal of the vows made on their behalf by parents or sponsors. In this renewal exercise, they are being asked to recommit to their belief in the forgiveness of sins.

Form a circle. Pass the bowl of water to the person to your right with the invitation to dip his or her hands in the bowl of water as you say, "(Name), remember your baptism. Remember that God is willing to forgive your sins, both past and yet to come." That person then takes the bowl of water, passes it to the next person, and repeats similar words. Continue all around the circle. Invite everyone to say, "I believe in the forgiveness of sins. Thanks be to God!"

WRAPPING UP

Invite participants to revisit the questions they named at the beginning of the session about forgiveness of sin. Have some questions been answered to their satisfaction? Have other questions arisen? Remind participants that forgiveness is a central part of what Christians believe. When we say we believe in the forgiveness of sins, we are recognizing that we all need forgiveness, that God forgives us, and that we are called to forgive others.

Encourage participants to read Chapter 6 before the final session. Also ask them to reflect in the coming days on any wrong done to them that they have found it difficult to forgive. Encourage them to offer up that wrong to God, asking that they be released to forgive that person.

Closing Activity

Ask someone to again read aloud Matthew 6:14-15, found in the book chapter. Note that when we pray the Lord's Prayer, we are asking God to forgive us in the same way and to the same degree in which we forgive others who may have hurt us or done us wrong.

Invite participants to pray the Lord's Prayer together. Call attention to the spaces you left after the words *forgive us our trespasses*, and again after the words *as we forgive those who trespass against us*. Invite participants to pray silently after the first set of words, asking forgiveness for things they have done or left undone. After the second set of words, ask them to pray silently that they will be able to forgive persons who have wronged them. Following the second time of silence, continue to recite the prayer to the end.

Invite volunteers to respond to the following:

- In asking forgiveness of God, I feel a sense of _____.
- In forgiving those who have wronged me, I feel a sense of _____.
- With respect to forgiveness, I continue to need God's help in _____.

Closing Prayer

Invite participants to join in praying the traditional Anglican and Methodist prayer of confession, found in the book chapter:

Most merciful God,
we confess that we have sinned against you
in thought, word, and deed,
by what we have done,
and by what we have left undone.
We have not loved you with our whole heart;
we have not loved our neighbors as ourselves.
We are truly sorry and we humbly repent.... Amen.

6.

THE RESURRECTION OF THE BODY

PLANNING THE SESSION

Session Goals

As a result of conversations and activities connected with this session, group members should begin to:

- examine what the Bible says happens after death;
- explore what the Bible says about resurrection of the body and the final judgment;
- consider ways in which beliefs influence how we face our own deaths and how we grieve the loss of those we love;
- affirm a commitment to believe, as articulated in the Apostles' Creed.

Creedal Foundation

I believe in . . .
> *the resurrection of the body*
> *and the life everlasting. Amen.*
>
> —*The Apostles' Creed*

Special Preparation

- Continue to have available copies of the ecumenical Apostles' Creed, or post it where all can see it, either on a large sheet of paper or a board. Alternatively, plan to project it.
- Also display the lines for today's session.
- On a large sheet of paper, draw the diagram of Hades/Sheol from the book chapter.
- Decide if you will do one of the optional activities. For creating prophetic signs, do an Internet search for cartoons with the title "The End Is Near" and print some out.
- You will also need large sheets of paper or posterboard and markers. If you will sing the hymn "Precious Lord, Take My Hand," participants will need smartphones to do an Internet search. Get the lyrics and arrange for singing or reciting the hymn.

Getting Started

Opening Activity

Welcome participants to this last session. Provide materials for those who do not have an electronic device for journaling.

Gather together. Remind participants that since the last session, they were to reflect on and pray about forgiving those who have wronged them. Without asking for details, ask volunteers to tell whether they were able to release that person—and themselves—by forgiving him or her.

Invite participants to respond to the following:

- What are some "hot button" issues some Christians today seem willing to fight over?
- Which ones do you consider essential to being a Christian?

Remind them that the purpose of the Apostles' Creed when it was first formulated was to offer a very short list of things that were considered essential to confess if one were to be baptized as a Christian. So many of the things that fuel conflict in the church today are not found in the Apostles' Creed, nor in any of the other creeds that date from the first five centuries of Christianity.

Tell the group that in this final session, they will consider the last of the essentials in the Apostles' Creed—the promised return of Christ, the last judgment mentioned earlier in the Creed, the resurrection of the body, and the life everlasting.

Opening Prayer

Loving God, we give thanks for your creating, saving, and sustaining presence in our lives. Guide us as we seek to understand more about your will for us, and for the life of the community of faith into which you have called us. Open our hearts and minds to new insights and a new commitment to you. Amen.

LEARNING TOGETHER

Video Study and Discussion

Chapter 6 explores what we believe about what Adam Hamilton calls the great existential crisis every human being must face: death.

To set the scene for viewing the video, ask participants to consider the following:

- When did it first really hit you that we're all going to die, and that everyone we know and love is going to die?
- What were you thinking and feeling when this revelation first sank in?

After viewing the video, discuss some of the following:

- Hamilton notes that our fear of death leads us to go to some extraordinary lengths to prolong life. Are there other indications or aspects in our contemporary culture that you think point to a fear of death?
- What does he suggest is God's response to our mortality and to the grief God knows we will feel at the death of people we love?
- What is your response to what Hamilton has to say about what our resurrected bodies will be like?
- How does the Bible portray heaven?
- How does belief in the Resurrection change how you face life and death?

Tell participants that they will explore in more depth what happens after death, as well as the resurrection of the body, later in the session. Invite them to name questions they have about life after death, and jot these down.

Book Study and Discussion

Examine What Happens After Death

Invite volunteers to briefly summarize what the artifacts of early cultures tell us about their concept of life after death. Remind participants that in Chapter 2, the author gave us some information about the Jewish beliefs regarding what happens after death.

Ask volunteers to review the diagram you posted that shows how many Jews in Jesus' time pictured the afterlife. Note that what is labeled as Tartarus on the diagram was also known as Gehenna, the term the Adah Hamilton used in Chapter 2.

Ask volunteers to read aloud the following verses included in the book chapter: 1 Corinthians 15:6, 54; 2 Corinthians 5:1; John 11:25-26; John 14:19. Discuss:

- In quoting Paul Tillich, the author tells us that the Resurrection is God's response to the frightful presence of death. How does the Resurrection change how you view death?

Remind participants that the Bible portrays heaven as being like a joyous wedding reception. Ask someone to read the passage from Isaiah describing heaven, which is included in the book chapter. Ask:

- What do you imagine heaven to be like?
- What do you think death is like? Is the story of the dog whining at the door a helpful analogy for you? If not, can you describe what you hope the experience of dying will be like for you?

Explore the Final Judgment

Invite volunteers to read aloud the passages included in the book chapter about the final judgment (1 Thessalonians 4:16-17 and 2 Peter 3:8-10). A number of end-times prophets have wrongly predicted dates for the return of Christ in the last two hundred years. Discuss some of the following:

- What does Hamilton contend is the point of biblical texts affirming that Christ will return to judge the living and the dead?

- Hamilton observes that we should always be ready to meet Christ, and he notes ways we might do so. In what kinds of spiritual practices do you regularly engage that might keep you in a state of readiness?

Explore the Resurrection of the Body

Ask participants to scan the information in the book chapter under the heading "The Resurrection of the Body" and name some of the questions posed. Jot these down on a large sheet of paper or a board. To this list, add any other questions the group has. Then ask someone to read aloud the passage included in the book chapter (1 Corinthians 15:42-44, 54). Discuss:

- What can we infer about the resurrected body from Jesus' appearances to his disciples?
- What does the writer suggest that DNA might have to do with the resurrection of the body?
- What kind of body would you hope to have in resurrection?

More Activities (Optional)

Create Prophetic Signs About the Final Judgment

Distribute copies or project the cartoons you found that depicted the end-time. Ask participants to read over the cartoons and respond to them. Discuss:

- Why do you think these cartoons and jokes about the end-time are so funny?
- In your opinion, what is driving the need of some Christians to have a definitive answer for when Christ will come again?

72

- Invite participants to think about what they believe about the end-time and to create signs with slogans that illustrate that belief. When the signs are completed, ask participants to display them and give an explanation for the slogan they chose.

Sing or Recite a Hymn

Invite participants to do an Internet search to find the story of how Thomas Dorsey came to write the hymn "Precious Lord, Take My Hand." After participants report on the circumstances that led to Dorsey's writing the hymn, discuss:

- What was the shattering news Thomas Dorsey received that led to his writing this hymn?
- Have you ever received similar news about a loved one? How did you react? How did your faith sustain you?

Invite the group to sing or recite the hymn together.

Explore the Gospels's Witness to the Resurrection of the Body

Invite participants to explore what various accounts in the Gospels tell us about the resurrection of the body. Form small groups or pairs, and assign one of the following passages from John or Luke to each: John 20: 1-10; 20:11-18; 21:19-23; 20:24-29; 21:1-14; Luke 24:13-35; 24:36-42. After allowing a few minutes for them to read, ask:

- What indications are there in these passages that Jesus had a bodily presence after his resurrection?
- What indications are there that his body was in some way altered?

WRAPPING UP

Revisit the questions about the afterlife that participants posed following the video. Which questions have they answered, and which remain?

What we believe about death affects both how we face our own death and how we grieve the loss of those we love. Invite participants to reread the stories of eighty-seven-year-old Ben and of Hamilton's colleague Julie. Encourage them to continue to reflect on the following questions:

- How does my faith influence the way I face the reality of my own death?
- How does it impact the way I deal with the surety of the deaths of those I love?

Closing Activity

Invite participants to read silently and reflect on the words under the heading "An Invitation." Then emphasize that in the end we make a choice to believe. Ask them to write the open-ended prompt in their journals: "I choose to believe that..."

Encourage them to respond with what they believe about God, Jesus Christ, and the Holy Spirit.

About the lingering questions they may still have, invite them to respond to this prompt: "I commit to continued exploration and discernment about..."

Closing Prayer

Close by repeating the Apostles' Creed one final time. Then say the following prayer that closes the book:

O God, I trust that you exist and that the wonders of our universe are all your handiwork. Thank you for creating this planet on which we live with its capacity to sustain life. Thank you for creating human beings in your image and for making it possible for us to understand and acknowledge you as our Creator. Thank you for caring about us and for us.

Jesus Christ, thank you for the truth you came to reveal, the life you came to give us, the death you suffered for us, and for the resurrection by which you conquered evil, hate, sin, and death. I trust you as my Savior. Help me to follow you daily as my Lord.

Come, Holy Spirit, fill my heart. Form me and shape me as a potter shapes the clay. Transform my heart, sanctify me, and make me the person you intend me to be. Help me to love and to bear your fruit in my life.

Thank you, O God—Father, Son, and Holy Spirit. All that I am, I offer to you. Help me to live the words of the Creed and to incorporate their meaning into my daily life.

In Jesus' name.

Amen.

Notes

1. Karl Menninger, *Whatever Become of Sin?* (New York: Hawthorn Books, 1972), 188.

2. Paul Tillich, *The New Being* (New York: Scribner's, 1955), 9.